I. B. Galbraith
Beechwood
Overton Road
Alexandria
Dunbartonshire G83 0LJ

C000179483

On Glasgow & South Western Lines
David Cross

Right: The 22 June 1966 sees Standard Class 5 No 73101 slowly emerging from Barassie Works with the 'workers' train. Barassie was a large carriage and (particularly) wagon works which undertook repairs and refurbishment for the wagon fleet in southern Scotland. It was a large sprawling site and a portion of the works can be clearly seen in the picture to the right of the train. Like so many other railway sites, it is now a housing development. The use of such a powerful locomotive on such a short train gives a clear indication that the end of steam was nigh. A Standard Class 5 on a three-coach stopping train was unusual. After Barassie the next stop would be Gailes, followed by Irvine, Bogside Race Course and Kilwinning and then all stations to Glasgow, dropping off employees of the works all along the line. No 73101, clearly a 67A Corkerhill locomotive, was one of the Scottish Region Standard 5 fleet throughout its short life of just 12 years or so. *All photographs by Derek Cross*

Ian Allan
PUBLISHING

First published 2001

ISBN 0 7110 2795 1

Published by Ian Allan Publishing

an imprint of Ian Allan Publishing Ltd, Hersham, Surrey KT12 4RG.
Printed by Ian Allan Printing Ltd, Hersham, Surrey KT12 4RG.

Code: 0106/B1

Foreword:
Derek Cross — A Most Remarkable Gentleman

My first contact with Derek Cross was a formal request for his help to provide appropriate photographs for some covers of my Transacord LP and EP records. His equally formal response was immediate, and from then on he never failed to send a large selection of appropriate prints, for the use of which he courteously accepted a meagre fee, often accompanying its receipt with an increasingly hilarious message. When we eventually met in 1964 it turned out that on an August Bank Holiday Saturday in 1959 we had been within earshot of each other at Greenholme when I had been on the Tebay side of a bridge recording a procession of trains, while Derek and his son David had been photographing the same trains on the Shap side of a bridge, out of sight.

Subsequently, when the majority of Britain's railways became progressively and disgracefully run down, Ayrshire, as with the railways on the Continent, remained an oasis of living steam, efficiently and enthusiastically operated, with Derek's support and guidance, on lines such as the Ayr–Stranraer route and the Ayrshire colliery networks. The hospitality of the Cross family and Derek's guidance and assistance in making recordings were so much appreciated as a contrast to increasing horrors on other lines.

Derek knew every detail of the locations and operations on those railways; indeed, it seemed at times they were operating under his control or at least with his connivance! For instance, there was a colliery siding at Bargany which Derek suggested as a spectacular position for recording because of the difficulty which locomotives had when leaving the siding with a loaded train. A memorable, much published recording was made there of a 'Black 5' 4-6-0 which spent some 20 minutes raising echoes with violent bursts of slipping before moving out from the siding. Meanwhile, Derek stood in the road which led past the siding and managed to stop any vehicles from coming past the siding, so preserving the integrity of my recording.

Derek knew every detail of locations such as Kilmarnock and had considerable influence locally in the way that locomotives were allocated and driven in the Ayrshire area. His influence certainly extended to the PR departments when he helped me to get footplate recording permits for the double-headed Ayr–Stranraer boat train and later, in 1967, for a footplate journey on a '9F' between Carlisle and Hellifield, a recording of which has now been published.

Derek also achieved some fame in the film industry by providing me with some remarkable sound effects which were successfully used in the soundtrack of *The Charge of the Light Brigade*, but that is altogether a different story.

The only drawback to our Ayrshire recording adventures was the weather. For instance, even in mid-summer we spent an entire night at Glenwhilly attempting to make recordings in a howling gale and driving rain; the recordings were useless, which was a disappointment, but that, as always, was compensated by Derek's inimitable company: he was a truly remarkable gentleman, and the biggest disappointment of all was Derek's unexpected and untimely death.

Peter Handford

Introduction

There are numerous people still writing books in their early seventies and that really should be the case with my father, Derek Cross. His untimely death in 1984, as well as being a shock, left a vast collection of material in my possession, much unpublished, gnawing away at me to do something with it.

Each month I still get letters from members of the railway fraternity asking if I can help with a picture of a particular locomotive, often at a particular geographical location. I do my best to help and generally people are satisfied. The catalyst, however, to do something along the lines of this book, *On Glasgow & South Western Lines*, was when these requests turned to diesel! Until recently, such requests were nearly always for a photograph of *Clan Cameron* on Beattock Bank, the long-closed Maxwellton station or 'Royal Scot' *Honourable Artillery Company* at work in North Wales. Over the last 12–18 months, however, the requests have been for diesel-hydraulics, Claytons, green Class 40s and other more modern locomotives. The change in the requests from being mostly steam to mostly diesel made me think that if I did not do something soon there might be insufficient interest in steam to make the book the success I hope it will be. In order to take cognisance of what the market wants, I have included some early diesel pictures. I sincerely hope the steam-only readers will forgive this action. The photographs of diesels have been carefully selected, both for their interest and to help with the geographical scope of the book. The plain truth is that none of us are getting any younger, and what material Derek had I would like to share with you.

How Did It All Start?

The origins of Derek's interest in railways and railway photography were little more than an accident, as I suspect was the way for many people. Derek's interest was borne out of his frustration with fishing! As a teenager, immediately after the war, his lack of success with a rod on the River Urr, near Dalbeattie, caused his interest in fishing to wane. Where he was fishing was within sight of the Dumfries–Stranraer railway line, and Derek began to notice the Compounds and the 'Crabs' which passed from time to time. In fact, the first photograph he ever took of a steam engine was of Midland Compound No 40919 on a Stranraer to Dumfries train near Dalbeattie. It is interesting that the late Bill (W. J. V.) Anderson, a contemporary of Derek and co-author of the Ian Allan *Steam in Scotland* books, began in much the same way. He had been taken to an air show by his mother and paid no attention to the aeroplanes at all, preferring to watch the trains on a nearby railway line. He later went to school in Rugby where, as you can imagine, this fledgeling interest in steam quickly developed into a major fascination. Derek had gone to school in Scotland, but it was not really until his university days at Wye College in Kent, close to where he had been born in Hythe in the late 1920s, that his real interest in railway photography began.

A number of people have asked me what camera Derek used to take the bulk of his pictures. He started off with a Voigtlander Bessa camera which, over the

*Left:*Derek's first photograph of a steam engine: Midland Compound No 40919 on the 'Port Road' at Dalbeattie in April 1949.

gauge steam locomotives thundering past my pram! Apparently I wasn't frightened at all by the noise and sheer size of these roaring beasts. That, as they say, was that, and I guess that in order to see my father at all the best thing to do was to join him. My expeditions with him were a part of my upbringing that I remember vividly. In this country I suppose my first expedition with Derek took place when I was about seven years old. I remember my first ever night in an hotel took place at the George Hotel in Orton, a stone's throw from Shap. I remember thinking that the hotel was huge, that pineapple juice was a delicacy beyond imagination and what on earth was all the fuss about signing the visitors' book? I have been back to the hotel several times since and am always amazed to find only six rooms at most! My view of pineapple juice has thankfully changed. However, I wish very much now that I had the visitors' book because, one after the other, Messrs Anderson, Cross, Lockett, Peters and Treacy had signed in — exalted company indeed!

There were other advantages. I was always top of the class in geography, probably because of the amount of time we spent driving around the country in pursuit of steam trains. Between the ages of 7 and 15 I really enjoyed being the navigator, map reader, lunch-feeder and part time film-changer for my father at the same time as racing along narrow roads at great speed to get to the next shot! I'm surprised I survived in a world without seat belts!

Such adventures further included my first high-speed tyre blow-out (chasing 'Jubilee' *Sierra Leone* on the Settle & Carlisle!), my first brush with the police (they thought we'd abandoned the car whilst taking photographs on the Esk Viaduct at Mossband near Gretna) and my first beer (a lukewarm Mackeson, which was revolting!).

From a very young age I, too, had a camera, an Ilford Sporti, which consumed countless rolls of Selochrome Pan to little or no effect but was all

years, he upgraded, such that by the time we returned from New Zealand in 1958 he had progressed to a Linhof with easily interchangeable backs and lenses and some 35mm equipment. Much of the black and white material was taken on large format 2¼in x 3¼in negatives with eight frames to a 120-size roll film. Later, this evolved to 12 frames of 2¼in square format. Derek used the interchangeable backs for both colour and black and white photographs. The bulk of the large format material in this book was taken on Agfa CT 18 film. Later on, the Linhof was replaced by a Rollei SL66. The 35mm slides were taken either with a Leica or a Canon 7S. Much of the material was taken on Kodachrome One because at 25ASA it was the fastest film on the market during the 1960s — a major advance on the 8ASA Dufay colour of the 1950s.

We have talked about Bill Anderson and Derek getting the railway bug by accident or, more correctly, through frustration with other activities. I think in my own case I can safely say it was no accident! From a very early age in New Zealand, babysitting for me was done by dropping me off at the wayside station of Putararu on the outskirts of Roturua on the North Island of New Zealand. According to my mother, I seemed to enjoy viewing huge Glasgow-built 3ft 6in

Above: This archetypal 1960s Ayrshire picture sees 'Crab' No 42919 blasting its way through the cutting just north of Hollybush station on the early morning train of empty coal wagons. The train of up to 50 empty wagons originated at either Falkland Junction or Ayr Harbour and is en route to the NCB/BR interchange sidings at Waterside on the Dalmellington branch. By the time this picture was taken in September 1966 (just three weeks before steam ended) the passenger service had ceased and the line saw coal traffic only. As with several of the lines in Ayrshire depicted in this book, it is pleasing to report that the line remains open and still plays host to coal traffic.

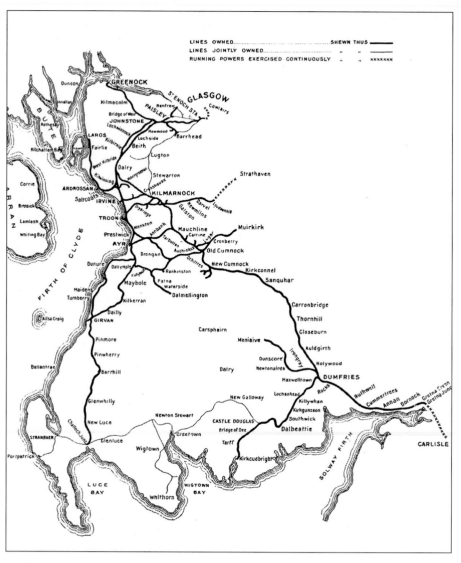

Above: Map of the G&SW issued with the Director's Report to the shareholders 1913 onwards. *Courtesy of the Stephenson Locomotive Society*

Right: The author aged 10 on 'Black 5' No 45158 *Glasgow Yeomanry* on a ballast train at Annbank in April 1964.

hugely enjoyable. The first time I saw the red Stanier Pacific No 46247 *City of Liverpool*, the match for my three-rail Hornby-Dublo model, at Carstairs was another memorable moment on expedition with Derek in southwest Scotland in the 1960s. There are other smaller things I recall vividly. In the days before 24-hour radio it was a thrill to hear the BBC Home Service crackle into life on the car radio with Handel's Water Music at 6.45am, then to drive through such a 'big town' as Dumfries in darkness and see only milkmen and to race across the border past Gretna Green to be at Carlisle Kingmoor for breakfast. Once there we would see both what interesting workings were diagrammed and what the weather was set to do. Depending on the answer to that last important question, a decision was made as to whether to go on to Penrith or back to the Dumfries/Lockerbie area.

Little did Derek imagine that 15 years after his death I would be putting together this album. I don't suppose for a moment he appreciated the indelible impression that those formative years in the 1960s would have on me. I don't think he realised the variety of traffic and beauty of the countryside that southern Scotland held or indeed the valuable historical record he was creating.

The LMS and Shap, in particular, were his favourites but he had soft spots for other areas such as the Somerset & Dorset and, perhaps strangely for a landscape photographer, areas of South London and north Kent. He requested that his ashes be scattered at Shap Wells and this was duly done. A headstone in his memory is now part of the graveyard at the little village church of St Michael in Shap. Quite how these things happen I don't know, but as the ashes were being scattered the electric locomotive *Stephenson* went past. It was ironic because some of the pictures in this book are of the Stephenson Locomotive Society specials which so characterised Easter-time in Scotland in the 1960s.

This book is very roughly a geographical trek through southwest Scotland during the years between 1959 and 1970, on lines over which the Glasgow & South Western Railway originally ran. Glasgow, the Clyde Coast, Ayrshire, the line to Stranraer, the 'Port Road' between Dumfries and Stranraer and the former G&SW Nith Valley line make up the route.

I apologise if not all the detail is completely accurate, my defence being that I was only 12 when the hub, the steam shed at Ayr, closed. It was all great fun, and I hope you also enjoy the experience my father and I shared.

David Cross

5

The city of Glasgow, in view of its large industrial base and population, had been much fought over in terms of access by the pre-Grouping companies. This had resulted in four large termini: Glasgow Central, Glasgow Queen Street, Glasgow Buchanan Street and Glasgow St Enoch. Add to these a plethora of suburban stations and the first electric underground system in the UK and you had a most comprehensive pre-mass-motor car suburban rail system. Glasgow St Enoch essentially served the Clyde coast lines and the former Glasgow & South Western lines. Always a station associated with tank engines, this picture of Standard tank No 80008 entering the station on 19 September 1962 proves the point! The train is a semi-fast from Ardrossan to Glasgow. The advent of both diesel and electric multiple-units greatly reduced the need for large stations and as a result the stations at Buchanan Street and St Enoch closed in the 1960s, leaving the present-day Glasgow Central (serving the south) and Glasgow Queen Street (serving the north).

Right: The first serious gradient on the G&SW main line southbound from Glasgow St Enoch is the Neilston Bank. Just 14 miles from the end of the platform in Glasgow, locomotive and crew had to be in good shape if the first stop at Kilmarnock was to be reached on time. Different classes of locomotive had different load limits, the Stanier and Gresley Pacifics having the highest, down through 'Royal Scots' and 'Jubilees' to Class 5 timings. Clearly, the load for this Glasgow–Leeds–St Pancras relief was more than the train engine, a 'Jubilee', could manage and a Class 5 pilot was assisting the train. Normally this would be to either Kilmarnock or New Cumnock but sometimes all the way through to Carlisle. This picture, taken on Easter Monday (3 April 1961) shows 'Black 5' No 45010 piloting Scottish-based 'Jubilee' No 45669 *Fisher*, the train engine which would work through over the Settle and Carlisle to Leeds.

Right: The three most Scottish Stanier Pacific 'Duchesses', *Buccleuch*, *Atholl* and *Montrose*, were amongst the first of Stanier's masterpieces to be withdrawn in 1962. All allocated to 66A Glasgow Polmadie, they appeared to be usurped from their prestigious Anglo-Scottish passenger duties earlier than their English-based sisters which you will recall were withdrawn *en masse* at an accountant's whim in September 1964 — what a waste! Here we see *Duchess of Buccleuch* (No 46230) pulling away from a signal check at Caldwell, a wayside station exactly halfway between Kilmarnock and Glasgow on the former G&SW main line. The train is a modest parcels from Carlisle to Glasgow parcels station; the date is October 1961.

Above: With the famous shipyards of the River Clyde in the background two 'Black 5s', Nos 45479 and 44992, storm up the 1 in 70/1 in 98 between Greenock Prince's Pier and Upper Port Glasgow. By then this line had been singled beyond Kilmacolm and so locomotives running tender to tender were not uncommon. This eased the running round problems on reaching the mainline at Elderslie just south of Paisley. The train is a return excursion from Greenock Prince's Pier to Ayr, in May 1964.

Right: The suburban line from Glasgow to the Clyde coast was one of the very first to lose its steam service. Dubbed the 'Blue Trains', electric multiple-units took over working to Gourock and Wemyss Bay in the early 1960s. Again, the line west of Paisley is not one widely photographed so although not a G&SW line I have included this picture taken near Langbank, on the south bank of the River Clyde, on 13 April 1970. Crossing shots are never easy to get but Derek appears to have managed getting the north bank town of Dumbarton between a Glasgow to Gourock EMU and a northbound engineer's train to Glasgow. Hauling the latter train is BRCW Type 2 diesel No D5408, recently transferred to Scotland from the London area, as part of the steam replacement.

Left: Pictured at Stewarton, the second station out of Kilmarnock, is a Kilmarnock–Glasgow St Enoch stopping train crossing the viaduct just south of the station. The date is 20 March 1963 and the locomotive Stanier 'Black 5' No 44718.

Above: Steam had almost gone from Ayrshire when this December 1966 picture was taken. Both the main sheds, at Hurlford (67B) and Ayr (67C), had recently closed to steam. Ex-LNER 'B1' No 61278 is seen departing southwards from Kilmarnock on an enthusiasts' special from Edinburgh to Carlisle which, I think, returned over the then-threatened Waverley route from Carlisle via Hawick to Edinburgh. At that stage there were four Anglo-Scottish main lines across the border: via the Nith Valley, the

Clyde Valley, the ECML via Berwick-upon-Tweed, and the Waverley route. For much of their working lives in Scotland the 'B1s' were associated with the former LNER lines; however, 'B1s' at Kilmarnock were not unknown. In January 1963 eight of the class had been allocated to Ayr (the first five of which were Nos 61007, 61134, 61243, 61261 and 61396 — made redundant by diesel traction in the east and north of Scotland). Essentially mixed traffic locomotives, the 'B1s' did not cope well with the steeply graded Ayrshire coalfield branches. The crews said that although the 4-6-0s had plenty of power, they were essentially passenger locomotives and their brakes in particular were not suitable for unfitted coal trains on steeply graded branch lines.

This August 1966 scene sees 'Britannia' No 70034 *Thomas Hardy* about to set off northbound from Kilmarnock with the morning mail and parcels service from Carlisle to Glasgow. By this time 'Britannias' had been relegated from front-line passenger work to reliefs, parcels/mail traffic and extra workings. The Glasgow autumn holiday excursions during the next month, September 1966, were the last year of steam dominance on such trains and it is reported that no less than 12 of the class worked into Scotland on one day during that month. Passing *Thomas Hardy* is Standard Class 4 2-6-0 No 76102 on local trip working A78 — perhaps on its way to the famous Johnnie Walker whisky sidings adjacent to the station in Kilmarnock.

The 'Britannia' had been delivered new to Manchester Longsight in December 1952. In 15 short years it saw varied use on a number of different regions. In May 1953 it went to Stewarts Lane on loan before transfer to the Eastern Region at Stratford in June 1953. It passed to Norwich in February 1959, then to March in June 1961 before returning to the LMR at Willesden in April 1963. It was transferred to Crewe North in July 1964, Crewe South in April 1965 and Newton Heath in August 1965 before a final transfer to Kingmoor in May 1966. It was withdrawn on 6 May 1967 and scrapped by J. McWilliams of Shettleston in September 1967.

Steam had been gone for nearly five years when this photograph was taken on 15 May 1971. The diesel successors to steam were a variety of classes, mostly dismissed locally as 'English hand-me-downs'. I've missed out the adjective often applied to the beginning of the sentence which meant that none of the locomotives sent to Ayrshire to replace steam was new. What became Classes 20, 24, 26 and 27 had all seen use elsewhere before their arrival in southwest Scotland. BR/Sulzer Type 2 No D5002, photographed here on the same sort of mixed freight that steam had hauled for years previously, is seen wandering through the semaphores at the north end of Kilmarnock station. It is interesting to compare the relative lifespans of the locomotives. The 'Crabs' and 'Black 5s' had often worked for 30 years or more. This Sulzer was built in December 1958, stored in 1975 and cut up in 1977 — a working life of less than 20 years. This particular locomotive followed Derek around as he had photographed it on the London Midland Region, the Southern Region and here in Scotland.

13

Above: Barassie is probably more famous for its golf courses than for the railway wagon works and the always beautifully manicured garden on the triangular platform at the station! In railway terms Barassie was an important location in Ayrshire. It was firstly the junction for the line to Kilmarnock from the Ayr to Glasgow route, secondly, the junction for the Troon avoiding line (to Lochgreen Junction), and thirdly, an important wagon repair works for southwest Scotland. There was also a small yard there that serviced Troon Harbour. Troon Harbour, of course, in the shape of West of Scotland Shipbreakers, was the Scottish equivalent of Woodham's at Barry, where hundreds of locomotives (from *Duchess of Norfolk* to more modest 'Jinties') were scrapped in the period 1962 to 1967. Pictured here is Standard 2-6-0 No 77018 on an Ayr–Kilmarnock stopping train in the platform at Barassie. The June

1966 picture shows people alighting from the train in both directions: to the station exit next the locomotive and to the rear of the train — a short walk to the wagon repair shops. Shortly after the picture was taken the short-lived diesel rail buses took over this service.

Right: With the world-famous golf links at Troon on the left, where the Open Championship is played, we see Fairburn tank No 42122 make its way southwards towards Ayr in the summer of 1962. The train is a Kilmarnock to Ayr stopping train. The next stop is Prestwick, then Newton-on-Ayr before it reaches its destination at Ayr. Note the golfers on the track behind the train.

The steam days term of a 'filling-in' turn often meant the 'theft' of a locomotive from its regular diagram to cover for a shortage of power at the shed it was visiting. Here on 24 May 1964 we have photographic evidence! Carlisle Kingmoor (12A) 'Britannia' No 70007, complete with its *Coeur de Lion* nameplates, has just shunted an enormous rake of empty coal wagons into one of the reception sidings at Falkland Junction, the main yard for the Ayrshire coalfield immediately north of Newton-on-Ayr station. After taking water she would return light engine to Glasgow to take up her booked diagram, the shedmaster at Carlisle Kingmoor being none the wiser. This 'Britannia', once the pride of Norwich shed, had moved away from the Great Eastern in 1963 and just a year later found herself employed on moving coal empties — how quickly the mighty fell towards the end of steam. No 70007 was delivered new to the Great Eastern section in April 1951 for use on Norwich-Liverpool Street expresses and by August 1952 was allocated to Norwich, then transferred to March in November 1961. The locomotive was later stored at March before being transferred to Kingmoor in December 1963. It was withdrawn on 19 June 1965 and scrapped at Crewe the following month.

Right: For many years the seaside town of Ayr has been a
traditional holiday day out for the people of Glasgow. Before the
days of universal car ownership this meant that on most summer
weekends several relief trains ran from Glasgow to Ayr. Here on
3 August 1965 Standard tank No 80051 brings a Glasgow to Ayr
relief cautiously across the River Ayr, 100 yards from the platform
at Ayr. Motive power on these reliefs was extremely variable and
largely a question of what was on hand at Corkerhill shed in
Glasgow. The variety ranged from 'local' locomotives such as this
67A Standard tank to 'Duchesses', 'A3s' and 'Peak' diesels laying
over between Anglo-Scottish trains, stolen to answer the local cry
of 'nae poower'. The Standard tanks and their steam sisters had by
then been relegated to lesser duties and relief trains in favour of
early diesel and electric multiple-units. The train would have
begun its journey in Glasgow from St Enoch station, which at that
stage had less than a year's life left, closing on 27 June 1966.

Right: Crewe, Derby and Kilmarnock were all famous locomotive
works and here at Ayr on 5 October 1964 we see products of all
three crossing the River Ayr with a most unusual working. The
occasion was the movement of *Duchess of Sutherland* to the
Butlin's holiday camp at Heads of Ayr, a few miles south of Ayr.
The locomotive had been moved from Crewe, having been
cosmetically restored prior to going on display at the holiday
camp. She remained there for the next seven years to 1971, at
which time she moved to the Bressingham museum in Norfolk.
Heading this cavalcade were examples of Kilmarnock- and Derby-
built shunters, Nos D2434 and D3005 respectively hauling one of
Crewe's finest, two locomotives being required to help with
pulling and stopping such a heavy unbraked load. On the footplate
stands the former shedmaster at Ayr, Bill Bennett, a long-time
friend of Derek and a very pro-steam man right until the end of
Ayrshire steam in October 1966. He organised my first ever
footplate trip, at an age I won't mention in case I offend or shock
an HSE official! With *Duchess of Sutherland* coming to the end of
a most welcome and expensive restoration in Derbyshire this year
(2001), wouldn't it be nice to see her back in Scotland again,
probably at Ayr where she spent so much of her time north of the
Border?

17

Left: London, Brighton & South Coast visits Scottish West Coast! The date was 1 October 1964, and the imposing spire of St Leonard's Church in Ayr overlooks the transfer of 'Terrier' No 32662 (*Martello*) from rail to road. Once safely on the road vehicle she was moved the 4 miles or so to the Butlin's holiday camp at Heads of Ayr for static display. It and *Duchess of Sutherland*, pictured previously, shared a plinth there for the next seven years. No 32662 is now based at the Bressingham steam museum near Diss in Norfolk.

Above: Holbeck-allocated 'Peak' class diesel No D19 slowly propels the ECS (empty stock) of a race special from Glasgow to Ayr out of Ayr station in April 1964.

Ayr boasts the only Grade One racecourse in Scotland and even today still attracts a substantial number of 'punters' from Glasgow on race days. As can be seen from the coaching stock, virtually anything serviceable in Glasgow would do for such excursions! The interesting thing about such race specials was that any form of motive power could, and usually did, turn up. For a 10-year period 'Duchesses', 'Royal Scots', 'Jubilees', Holbeck 'A1s'/'A3s', or even 55A diesels as seen here, meant Ayr station on race days was a must. The use of such varied power was because many of the express locomotives often laid over in Glasgow between Anglo-Scottish turns during the day and were 'borrowed' for the hour or so journey to Ayr or the other (now closed) racecourse at Bogside, near Irvine.

Left: Steam, diesel and now electric, Ayr station has changed very little in over 50 years. Dominated by the Station Hotel, even the advent of electrification has not materially altered the pleasing open appearance of this important commuter station. Pictured during the morning of 5 July 1966 we see two 'Black 5s', Nos 44726 and 44925, ease through the station with the Stranraer–Glasgow mail and parcels service. By that stage two steam locomotives, steam and diesel, or two diesels could be the motive power for this daily service.

Above: Steam in Ayrshire had ceased in 1966 and logic suggests that the 1964-built diesels that replaced the steam locomotives should have lasted rather longer than seven years. However, some of the early diesels in this country were spectacularly unsuccessful and the Clayton Type 1s came pretty close to the top of that league. In this picture, taken on 27 March 1972, the former busy steam shed at Ardrossan (67D), which closed in September 1969, has been put back into somewhat unexpected use, the Scottish Region needing somewhere to put these unsuccessful diesels. In southwest Scotland they had been tried singly, in pairs, and with brake tenders — all to no avail, such that 20 or so examples were dumped at Ardrossan. Pictured here, left to right, are Nos D8573/D8531/D8515, all built 1963/4 and all withdrawn in 1971 after just seven years' poor service. Derek used to quip, 'Such is progress!'

Above: Preserved steam in southwest Scotland has never been big. Apart from, of course, the Scottish Region's four preserved pre-Grouping locomotives which had been such a success in the early 1960s, the occasion of the great Ayr open day of 1983 which brought *Flying Scotsman*, *Duchess of Hamilton* and *Maude*, and the emerging industrial museum at Minnevey are about the sum total. Unexpectedly, however, former LNER 'D49' 'Hunt' class No 246 *Morayshire* (BR No 62712), built in 1927, turned up at the ICI works at Ardeer near Saltcoats for storage in the summer of 1966. The background to this movement or indeed why the locomotive was stored at Ardeer is unknown to me. Ayrshire saw many locomotive types at work but never this particular class, new to the county in 1966!

Right: A long train of empty wagons destined for Killoch colliery climbs up the grade between Ayr and Annbank at Mossblown behind Hughes/Fowler 'Crab' No 42745. It never seemed to make much difference to the crews whether the locomotive was boiler first or tender first except on the Dalmellington branch, which always had the locomotive boiler first up the hill. Some said an important criterion was which direction the rain and wind were coming from on the day! Taken in the spring of 1961, this photograph also highlights the varied nature of Ayrshire agriculture, with hay or silage being harvested — it was not all Ayrshire cows and sheep. I also remember a couple of very large, friendly horses which sometimes came to see what the photographers were doing, and on occasions got so close to Derek that the shot was ruined! Mossblown had in the past been a junction for a line that went back to join the Ayr–Glasgow line at Monkton Junction.

Above: The early spring of April 1963 sees Standard 4 2-6-0 No 76096 at Mossblown between Annbank and Ayr. The broadside view shows the somewhat unattractive lines of the Riddles Standard locomotives but also illustrates the ease of maintenance not always evident in earlier former LMS locomotives: all moving parts are both visible and accessible, so reducing cost and time out of service. No 76096 and its sisters 76097/8 were allocated to Ayr for much of their short working lives (12 years or thereabouts) and could be found undertaking all manner of work — passengers, parcels, shunting and, as in the picture, the Littlemill Colliery to Ayr Harbour coal train.

Right: Annbank is one of those stations named after a town some distance away. Although much closer to the village of Mossblown, it has always been known as Annbank Junction even when it had a passenger service. Even today it is still a junction (of two single lines) and is still known as Annbank. In 1963 Annbank was a busy junction in the heart of the Ayrshire coalfield. Pictured on 8 June 1963 is Ayr-based Hughes/Fowler 'Crab' No 42805 drawing to a stand on the 'branch' platform. The train of loaded 16-ton coal wagons had originated from Whitehill Colliery and was destined for Ayr Harbour. With the link from the G&SW line at Mauchline to Ayr being the 'mainer' of the two lines, it is likely the coal train had had to yield. The length of train suggests that the opportunity to 'pin down' some wagon brakes would be taken before the descent to the coast at Ayr.

Left: For many years the 'Caley' 0-6-0s were the mainstay of the Ayrshire coalfield. By the late 1950s 'Crabs' and Class 5s had taken over the bulk of the duties; however, one daily working remained known locally as 'The Twins' because two identical locomotives always worked the daily coal train to Littlemill Colliery situated some 14 miles south of Annbank. The reason this working required 'Caley' 0-6-0s as opposed to larger motive power was the severe weight restriction on one of the bridges on the Littlemill branch. Here we see No 57644 leading its sister, No 57601, out of Annbank on the return journey to Falkland Junction in Ayr with the loaded wagons, on 5 May 1961. As with many Ayrshire collieries it was empties up, a shunt and loaded traffic down to the coast. For the few years between the demise of the Caley 0-6-0s and the end of steam, Standard Class 4 2-6-0s in the 76xxx series took over the Littlemill Colliery service. Some of you may remember Derek's 1961 Sunbeam Alpine (919 NKP) on the right of the photograph.

Below: A typical Ayrshire coalfield with a dirty Ayr-allocated Stanier 'Black 5' No 45160 restarting from a signal check immediately east of Annbank Junction. Derek records the empty coal wagons as being destined for the Barony colliery. Head first or tender first, 'Black 5' or 'Crab', it didn't really matter as long as the NCB got its empties and Northern Ireland its coal — that was the Ayrshire coalfield in the 1950s and 1960s. The white stripe on the leading wagon indicates a vacuum-braked vehicle as opposed to a plain unbraked wagon which, at that time, made up the majority of the fleet. A fitted head of a few vacuum-braked wagons next to the locomotive considerably enhanced the brake force of the train and so allowed a heavier payload to be moved.

Above: BR steam in southwest Scotland already gone when this picture of NCB No 2 was pictured at Barony Colliery in August 1967. The locomotive at that stage was a mere 82 years old, having been built by Nielson back in 1885. Engaged in shunting duties at the colliery transfer sidings, the old lady was feeding BR diesels (English Electric Type 1s — Class 20s) some 75 years younger! She soldiered on with her sister No 4 until the early 1970s before being scrapped.

Right: Snow in southwest Scotland is not common, it being both low lying and on the Gulf Stream-protected West Coast. However, on the morning of 1 March 1965 there had been a substantial overnight fall of snow. 'Black 5' No 45160, a local Ayr

(67C)-allocated engine, is seen approaching Drongan station with a loaded coal train from Killoch colliery to Ayr Harbour. The coal in all likelihood is destined for Northern Ireland. The line through the long-closed Drongan station still exists today and, although it is no longer a junction, modern-day coal trains still make their way past to Killoch, the most obvious difference being the always black locomotives have given way to the red, grey and blue locomotives of today. Although Killoch has closed as a colliery, its new status is that of a disposal point which sees locally mined open-cast coal brought in by road, then washed and loaded on to trains for transport to Irish, English and Scottish power stations, all much as it was in the 1960s, routed first to Falkland Junction and/or Ayr Harbour, just north of Ayr.

Below: Midland '4F' 0-6-0s were not common in Ayrshire; however, for many years Ayr had two of that type, Nos 44331 and 44390. Pictured leaving Drongan on the single-line branch to Littlemill is No 44390, struggling up the bank with a long rake of coal empties destined for Littlemill Colliery. Always an 0-6-0 working, in view of weight restrictions on the branch, the train was usually a 'Caley' 0-6-0, occasionally the Midland '4F' and rarely a 'J37' which Ayr also had during this summer of 1962.

Right: The local goods that pottered around the rail-connected industrial and foundry sites of Ayr was always known locally as the 'Squib'. Derek said that the 'Squib' was named such on account of its darting in and out of sidings, a constant annoyance to more important trains, signalmen and control. Towards the end of this service dedicated to only the odd wagon, Derek famously said the service was 'a misery to itself and a burden to others'! Anyway, in this picture of Ivatt 2-6-0 No 46482 taken on Monday, 5 April 1965 we see the fuel for the boilers at Glengall psychiatric hospital being delivered. This short siding left the main Ayr–Stranraer line at Glengall Junction between Alloway Junction (for Heads of Ayr) and Dalrymple Junction (for Waterside and Dalmellington). Towards the end, the signalmen often travelled with this weekly service (MO) and opened the signalbox, let the train in and reversed the procedure when the train departed. The stories of what went on within Glengall with the shunt are many; suffice to say, the driver and guard had to be very clear who was waving to whom! More than once the doors of the boiler house were damaged or wagons derailed by a wave from an unauthorised source from within the hospital as opposed to from British Railways employees!

Left: The morning coal empties from Ayr Harbour to the NCB complex at Waterside near Dalmellington, some 15 miles southeast of Ayr, was, on a fine morning, one of Derek's favourite Ayrshire coalfield workings along the Dalmellington branch. Many good locations, the light in the right place, varied motive power and a ruling gradient of 1 in 100 all helped him to reach this decision. Here we see local trip A36 leaving the Ayr–Stranraer line, visible in the background, at Dalrymple Junction and starting along the single line to Hollybush, Patna and Waterside. Motive power on this March morning in 1964 is Ayr-based 'Crab' No 42801. The 'Crabs' were the preferred power for this line and indeed throughout the Ayrshire coalfield. The crews preferred them to 'Black 5s', Standard Class 4s and 5s and the ex-LNER 'B1s' which were deemed to be reasonable pullers but much less adequate in the braking department. At this time when most trains were loose-coupled, and some had a fitted head either way, the 'Crabs' were the first choice motive power. These locomotives, although long associated with Ayr shed and Ayrshire, had themselves been cascaded (to use a modern word)

from the Highland lines. No 42801 in the early 1950s had been shedded at Forfar (63C).

Below: Northern Ireland provided much traffic for the railway of southwest Scotland, and this photograph, taken 2 July 1966, is confirmation. I recall the evening picture clearly; it followed a familiar pattern. A late afternoon phone call was received at home that a motor car special was to run from the Rootes car factory at Linwood, near Paisley, to Stranraer with cars for Northern Ireland. Plans were made, the weather looked at, an early dinner taken, the position chosen, the cameras checked and the ETD planned. Derek and I would often guess the motive power as we journeyed to Dalrymple Junction, under 5 miles from home. from the limited funds of a 12 year old I wagered a shilling on a 'Britannia' — how wrong I was! The train was actually hauled by English Electric Type 4 No D369, a mere 5 years old at that time. The fact that this then-new locomotive has now been withdrawn for 18 years confirms my observation in the Introduction that we are all getting older!

Below: The Dalrymple Viaduct was the only structure of any note on the Dalmellington branch which left the Ayr–Stranraer Line at Dalrymple Junction some 3 miles south of Ayr. Pictured in the high summer of July 1961, hence the lack of exhaust, 'Crab' No 42879 heads south along the single line with a rake of coal empties from Falkland Junction for the BR/NCB interchange sidings at Waterside. Locomotives tended to work head first up the branch with empties and tender first down the branch with loaded trains. They were allowed 50 empties up the hill and 36 loaded wagons down the steeply graded branch back to Ayr Harbour. At this time much of the coal was exported to Northern Ireland through the then British Transport Docks Board-owned harbour at Ayr.

Right: Photographers all have different views as to the best time of year to take photographs. In that regard Derek was at the conventional end of the spectrum and chose generally to have the train forming part of the landscape'. His formal training as a geologist, I always felt, had something to do with this. The two pictures here provide an interesting contrast between winter and summer. Both pictures are taken at Polnessan, a hamlet just north of Patna on the branch to Dalmellington and Waterside. Both feature the morning train of empty wagons from Ayr Harbour to NCB Waterside. The winter shot, with the snow, was taken in February 1962 with 'Crab' No 42800 making its way up the hill. This compares to the summer shot in the August 1966 view of similar locomotive No 42919 taken from the same spot.

Left: Once more we see a long train of coal empties blasting its way up the Dalmellington branch to the NCB interchange siding at Waterside. Ayr-based 'crab' No 42919 is seen passing the site of Holehouse Junction in the summer of 1965. Holehouse Junction had been a junction for a branch off the Dalmellington branch back to Rankiston. Closed in the 1960s, it was reopened for the first mile and a half in the late 1990s to allow opencast coal to be loaded at the Broomhills site. I am greatly encouraged, I am sure Derek would have been, that, no matter how slowly, bulk freight is making a return to rail transport. The ease with which the railway line was reinstated after over 30 years out of use is a tribute to the way those who built these branches a century ago constructed them. The reinstatement of this line on a junction which faces south means that it is one of the few modern air-braked freight trains which still use a brake van! The brake van is large, has bogies and is painted red, but I'm sure that Derek would have approved of this 'proper' complete freight train.

Above: This scene on 4 May 1964 shows the last train from Dalmellington (to Ayr) leaving the little terminus at Dalmellington. The train had been specially strengthened to two coaches but seems neither full nor leaving with any great fuss. This may have been just the reason that the line was being closed, there being no passenger interest in Dalmellington! The short section between Dalmellington and Waterside, the next station down the line, was closed and lifted shortly thereafter. The line beyond Waterside, where the NCB complex was located, remained open for freight traffic. The locomotive on this sad occasion was BR Standard Class 3 No 77016, itself destined to remain in traffic for only two more years. No 77016 was built in 1954 and allocated to 67B Hurlford (Kilmarnock) in its latter days, being withdrawn from there in March 1966. Stored at Hurlford until May 1966, it was scrapped by the Motherwell Machinery & Scrap Co of Wishaw in June 1966.

Above: For car enthusiasts the blue vehicle is a 1960 MG Magnette. Derek had a phobia about getting cars in his pictures. However, closer examination of his collection reveals that all of his cars have been included in the odd picture! In this book we feature two! Ah, the train! The National Coal Board (NCB) railway system above the Ayrshire town of Dalmellington was extensive, interesting and outlived BR steam in Scotland by over 10 years. The hills around Dalmellington were rich in minerals, with iron ore and coal both much in evidence. The nature of these products led to the establishment of several standard gauge industrial railway lines dotted all over these Ayrshire hills, going to exotically named locations such as Minnevey, Pennivenie and the Laight dump. The postwar NCB system was purely for coal mined in the hills then brought down to the washers at Waterside, which were connected to the BR network. The NCB divided Scotland into areas and this area was known as the West Ayr Area, which was written on the tank sides of each locomotive. Pictured at Minnevey with some NCB empty wagons heading for the loading point is Barclay 0–6–0ST West Ayr Area No 22 built in Kilmarnock in 1953. The distances travelled, in addition to the steep gradients, meant that all locomotives used a smaller coal wagon as a tender, clearly seen in this picture taken in 1962.

Right: BR steam had been gone from southwest Scotland for 12 years when this photograph was taken in 16 July 1978. With the main producer of industrial locomotives in Scotland, Andrew Barclay and Co, based just 25 miles away at Kilmarnock, it was no surprise that the bulk of the locomotives (or 'Pugs', as they were known locally) were from that stable in both 0-4-0ST and the more powerful 0-6-0ST varieties. NCB Barclay 0-6-0 No 24 was an interesting locomotive; apparently not a good steamer originally, she was fitted with a Giesl ejector chimney which moved her from the bottom to the top of the performance league overnight. This photograph shows the wagon tender to good effect as No 24 pulls away from the colliery sidings back on to the NCB main line on the right. The background of green hillsides is also an unusual backdrop to an industrial rail network. That same background is now host to an emerging steam preservation centre, under the Scottish Industrial Railway banner, recently opened on the site of the former colliery at Minnevey. One of the West Ayr Area Barclay 0-4-0STs is happily now back in residence in steam there.

In the modern railway everything seems to be uniform throughout the country and, as a result, less interesting. The word 'rare' is not much used. However, in the 1960s, when locomotives operated much more locally to their home depots, rare workings did occur, and Stanier '8F' No 48536, pictured here at Alloway Junction south of Ayr on the Stranraer line, falls into the extremely rare category. Stanier '8F' 2-8-0s were uncommon in Scotland generally, and exceedingly so in southwest Scotland. Carlisle Kingmoor-allocated 12A '8F' No 48536 is over 100 miles away from its home shed, being seen heading south of Ayr on the Chipmans 'weed-killer' train. Returning from Stranraer, the train, which Derek was most excited about, came back north again during darkness, so photography was not possible. Alloway Junction was the junction for the Heads of Ayr branch, formerly the Maidens & Dunure Light Railway, which goes off to the left beside the locomotive. The photograph was taken during May 1961.

In this view in summer of 1962 we see Stanier 'Black 5' No 44723 tender first on the empty coaching stock (ECS) for the Saturday-only working from Heads of Ayr to Edinburgh. The ex-LNER coaching stock gives an additional clue as to the destination. Pictured at Alloway Junction, leaving the Ayr to Stranraer line some 2 miles south of Ayr, the train would reach the Butlin's holiday camp Heads of Ayr station some 15 minutes later, where the locomotive would run round before setting off for the Scottish capital.

Left: On 31 March 1965 Ayr-based 'Black 5' No 45161 passes Dalrymple Junction signalbox and takes the Girvan Valley line towards Girvan and ultimately Stranraer. The line coming in from the right is the branch to Waterside and Dalmellington which joined the Girvan Valley line at this busy junction, approached from either side on gradients of 1 in 70 and 1 in 90. The train is the daily 'pick-up' from Falkland Junction to Girvan, where a leisurely shunt and lunch would be taken before returning to Ayr. No 45161 was the easiest to identify of the Ayr 'Black 5s' on account of its shining smokebox sustained over many years, the reasons for which were never clear to us!

Above: 1961/2 saw the end of steam working south of Ayr on regular passenger services to Girvan and Stranraer. Just south of Maybole there was a short gradient (of 1 in 63) known locally as the Crosshill Bank. In this picture taken in the summer of 1962 we see Standard Class 5 No 73123 approaching Maybole at the top of the

Crosshill Bank on a Girvan to Glasgow St Enoch working. After leaving Maybole the train has an easy downhill run over the nine miles to Ayr, and a further easy run in gradient terms over the following 41 miles to Glasgow. The most taxing part of the journey north of Ayr was the number of station calls to be made. A Girvan–Glasgow train, after Ayr, would probably stop eight times before reaching Glasgow in 75 minutes. Maybole was the closest station to our home and so often, if the phone rang advising of an interesting working on the Stranraer line, we could be at Maybole in less than 10 minutes. Sometimes, if the working was very unusual or the weather very good, we could, and did, get there faster at the expense of other road users! In these modern days of much increased car usage and road congestion I wonder how Derek might have coped. I'm sure many readers can imagine, and I fear that neither Derek nor Bill Anderson would have obtained the great number of pictures they did.

Below: The highly arable nature of South Ayrshire is visible all around in this picture of Stanier Class 5 No 45167 working hard up the Crosshill Bank (1 in 63) between Kilkerran and Maybole on the Girvan Valley line. The date is 8 August 1965 and the train is the afternoon northbound coal train from the pit at Bargany to Ayr Harbour. With 16 wagons and the brake van this was the maximum load for this line with a Class 5 locomotive. Because this line was shared with the Stranraer–Glasgow passenger service, attention to details such as loading was much more in evidence than on the freight-only branches.

Right: By June 1966 steam had just four months to go in Ayrshire and an element of decay has set in. 'Crab' No 42908, for so long the shedmaster at Ayr's pet locomotive, has become less looked after and much less clean. Although the signalbox at Dailly is still standing, by then it was 'switched out' for long periods, the other boxes down the Girvan Valley regulating the traffic. Kilkerran had the level crossing and Bargany the mine sidings, Maybole the goods yard, and as a consequence the need for Dailly, as traffic fell, was much reduced. In the foreground we can see the goods yard had already long been lifted. Some locomotives came to Ayrshire from other sheds indeed one of the Ayr 'Crabs' had been transferred from Huddersfield. No 42908, however, had been allocated to Dumfries (then 68B) as far back as 1949, gravitating within southwest Scotland to Ayr by 1963.

Below right: Restarting after a signal check at Bargany signalbox (seen on the right above the middle of the train) is the morning Stranraer–Glasgow parcels train. On the left is the reason for the signalbox, the NCB mine at Bargany, by then the only one in the Girvan Valley. The famous 'hole' that locomotives had such difficulty with when drawing loaded wagons out of the pit on a wet rail (ie often in Ayrshire) is on the left. Peter Handford in his foreword describes various goings-on at this favourite Derek Cross spot. The use of soap on the track was not unknown! Steam and diesel worked together for two to three years in Ayrshire and the picture, taken on 19 March 1966, shows that to good effect. The diesel, in this case No D5366, was always the pilot locomotive, whilst the train engine is Stanier Class 5 No 45477.

Below: North of Girvan the Girvan Valley line towards Ayr was quite steep in places, culminating in a short section of 1 in 60 between Bargany and Dailly. The first gradient of any note was the 1 in 72 through the long-closed station at Killochan, just two miles out of Girvan. Here in April 1965 we see long-time Ayr resident Stanier 'Black 5' No 45161 on a northbound train of coal empties. These empties could have been destined for the pit at Bargany colliery or perhaps were going straight through to the largest marshalling yard in the area at Falkland Junction just north of Ayr.

Right: In this June 1964 view we see 'Crab' No 42908 crossing the lesser of the two rail bridges over the famous fishing river, the Water of Girvan, just outside the seaside town of the same name. The main line crossed the river on a substantial stone bridge, whilst the single line to Girvan Goods crossed the river on this more flimsy structure. No 42908 is engaged in some shunting before setting off back to Ayr with the daily pick-up goods. This locomotive was often confined to out-and-back duties from Ayr shed (67C). Always kept clean, she was the Ayr shedmaster's favourite for the last couple of years of steam in southwest Scotland.

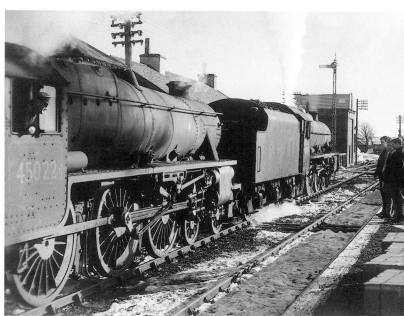

Above: The winter of 1963 was harsh throughout the UK, and southwest Scotland was no exception. The line to Stranraer had been blocked by snow at the Chirmorie summit between Barrhill and Glenwhilly and here we see a freight from Ayr to Stranraer at Barrhill awaiting a crossing with a northbound passenger. Evidence of the hard winter and snow are still to be seen as 'Black 5' No 45022 and 'Jubilee' No 45588 *Kashmir* sit in the platform. The novelty of any sort of train after the line being blocked appears to have brought out the locals for a look. Perhaps they were merely admiring the named 'Jubilee', unusually both used as a pilot and on a fitted freight. Immediately after leaving Barrhill the train climbed 4 miles at 1 in 67 up to the Chirmorie summit before descending to Glenwhilly and Dunragit where the 32-mile single-line section from Girvan ended.

Left: Steam ended in southwest Scotland when Ayr shed closed to steam on 3 October 1966. For about 2 years beforehand, steam and diesel had worked side by side, often together, as in this picture. Diesel availability was largely governed by cascade from other areas and, as the initial success of many early diesels in Scotland left a great deal to be desired in terms of reliability, planning must have been very difficult. The passenger turns were the first to be dieselised. A return working of the locomotive or locomotives that had headed into Stranraer during the night was the morning Stranraer to Glasgow parcels station mail and parcels service. Here seen crossing Pinmore Viaduct on the morning of 25 March 1966 is that train headed by BRCW Type 2 diesel No D5366 piloting Standard Class 5 No 73145, a Caprotti valve-geared variant. This section of the Stranraer line is single at this point and more or less immediately after the viaduct which twice crosses the A714 road the line passes into Pinmore tunnel.

Pausing at Barrhill on 24 June 1966 are a pair of 'Crabs', Nos 42863 and 42803, on an Irvine to Stranraer ballast train, taking a breather after their exertions up Glendoune Bank from Girvan. The strenuous efforts have had an effect on the smokebox door of No 42863 which is positively glowing! With neither locomotive in great condition (towards the end of steam, maintenance became cursory, at best), their efforts from Girvan had been slow. Derek has pictures of the train at Girvan, on the Glendoune Bank, at Pinmore, at Pinwherry and here at Barrhill. Five pictures in 10 miles tells its own story.

Left: The great freeze of winter 1963 is still in evidence, not only by the snow on the ground but also because steam is still in charge of the Glasgow–Stranraer trains. The cold weather had had a severe impact on the DMUs which by that time had taken over the passenger services — they could not cope with the weather at all! Enter Standard Class 5 No 73009, pulling away from the stop at Barrhill with a Glasgow–Stranraer train in February 1963.

Below left: Apologies to those of you who may have seen this picture before, but it was one of Derek's favourites of the Scottish preserved locomotives. On the evening of 15 April 1963 we see Highland Railway Jones Goods No 103 leading Great North of Scotland Railway No 49 *Gordon Highlander*, approaching Glenwhilly from the Stranraer direction. After crossing a Glasgow–Stranraer DMU, the train, the 1963 SLS Scottish Easter Tour, will set off northwards to Girvan, Ayr and Glasgow. I make no apology for the lack of words in this caption: it is simply the best of Scottish steam on Glasgow & South Western lines in the 1960s.

Below: Steam was still around in South Ayrshire when this picture was taken on 31 May 1966. We see Swindon-built diesel multiple-unit leaving Stranraer Harbour station with the 7.35am Stranraer–Glasgow St Enoch service. The ship in the background is the *Caledonian Princess*, a long-time participant on the car ferry service between Stranraer and the Northern Irish port of Larne. Because the railways in Ireland are of a different gauge, the concept of a train ferry to Ireland was never considered. The green hydraulic DMUs were very much part of the 1960s scene in southwest Scotland and I include this picture because there are some locations of which no one appears to have colour pictures, Stranraer Harbour being one such. There was another station at Stranraer (now closed) called Stranraer Town, which was adjacent to the locomotive depot.

Left: Easter time in Scotland in the early 1960s was nearly always time for an RCTS or SLS 'bash' around the country and April 1963 was no exception. That year, with the threat of Beeching, many of the lines in southwest Scotland were at risk. Many of these were covered using some of the Scottish preserved locomotives as well as locomotives in normal service. Pictured leaving Newton Stewart station on 15 April 1963 is 'Caley' '2F' No 57375 on the Isle of Whithorn leg of the tour to Whithorn and the Garlieston branch. Five bogie coaches was about the biggest single train these light railways ever handled. Behind the last coach the small locomotive shed at Newton Stewart, a subshed of Stranraer (68C), can be seen. Sadly, the whole railway system between Dumfries and Stranraer, including the branches, all closed just over two years later. Circumstances for locomotives changed quickly as well: No 57375, here all spruced up and on a passenger train, was photographed again by Derek just 13 months later (in black and white) being towed with its sister No 57355 from Stranraer shed to its demise at West of Scotland Shipbreakers, Troon.

Above: By May 1964 when this picture was taken, the daily freight to the Isle of Whithorn had been cut back to three times a week. Worse still for Derek was the fact that the 'Caley' 0-6-0s, for decades the mainstay motive power, had given way to 'new' engines. Pictured is one of these 'new' engines, BR Standard 2-6-0 No 78016. Having been built at Darlington in 1954, it had just celebrated its 10th birthday. Originally allocated to West Auckland, it had been transferred to Motherwell (66B) in August 1963 and moved quickly on to Dumfries (67E) some two months later. The mid-week Wednesday service is pictured standing in the platform at Wigtown station, the largest centre of population on the line. South of Wigtown the line reached the junction station of Millisle. At Millisle the line divided into the Garlieston branch and the Whithorn branch. Neither very busy, the Whithorn line probably had more traffic, with agricultural produce (potatoes and milk) and farm machinery predominating.

This May 1964 view sees Standard 2-6-0 No 78016 in the platform of the long-since-closed (to passengers) station of Sorbie on the Isle of Whithorn. The characteristic former station house is obvious on the left; what is more unusual is the creamery on the right which dominated the old station at Sorbie. By this time the thrice-weekly branch goods provided a valuable means of getting material to and finished products away from the creamery. The 'pick-up' would go down to the terminus at Whithorn, via Millisle, before running round and retracing its steps back to Newton Stewart and the 'main' line, known locally as the 'Port Road', from Stranraer to Dumfries.

The 'Crewe of the Isle of Whithorn' was what Derek jokingly dubbed the junction station of Millisle!. With a port at Garlieston and a bustling market town at Whithorn, Millisle must at one time have been busier than it had become by May 1964. By then the signalbox appeared to be much too big for the three-times-a-week freight. Pictured is BR Standard 2-6-0 No 78016, setting off behind the signalbox for Garlieston. The line this side of the signalbox continued to Whithorn.

Above: A further picture of the SLS Easter Tour of Scotland in 1963. Pictured at Whithorn station, the terminus of the Whithorn branch, 18 miles south of Newton Stewart, we see 'Caley' 0-6-0 No 57375 arriving with its five-coach special train. The welcoming party is not large, indeed I recall Derek commenting that day that photographers outnumbered local people. This was perhaps no surprise as the passenger service to Whithorn had been withdrawn several years earlier. The layout of the station was typical of several similar country stations throughout Scotland, with the passenger side on the right and the freight/goods/cattle dock on the left. A picture for station modellers!

Right: The 'Port Road' from Stranraer to Dumfries was one of Derek's favourite lines. It had all his favourite ingredients: rugged scenery, single-line sections, a wide variety of goods and passenger traffic and, before its closure in 1964, a wide variety of motive power. There was, however, an added ingredient of friendly but competitive footplatemen. In those days accompanying footplatemen was relatively easy and Derek got to know the Ayr, Stranraer and Dumfries crews pretty well. I think the driver we see here awaiting the 'right away' from Creetown with Standard tank No 80119 is Driver McCann of Stranraer shed. The train was the 8.10am from Dumfries to Stranraer and the date 13 August 1964. There is a famous tale about Driver McCann who on one occasion, again with Derek as his footplate guest, was awaiting departure from Stranraer Harbour with a 'Clan' class Pacific on a Stranraer–Newcastle working. McCann, unhappy to have a pilot that day, Standard 4 No 76097 to Ayr, went forward to the Ayr men on the pilot and asked two questions: 'Do ye ken who I am?' and before a reply could be given, 'Can ye run?!' Without waiting for a reply he returned to *Clan Mackenzie*, set off and pushed the luckless pilot locomotive and its crew all the way to Ayr!

Above: Sitting in the platform at Creetown station, still boasting gas lamps, is Stanier 'Black 5' No 45053. The train is a Stranraer to Dumfries freight and it will be waiting there to effect a crossing with a westbound passenger train. Forty-seven miles of the 'Port Road' from Castle Douglas to Dunragit were single line so it was common to have trains wait in stations for crossings. Creetown station was located on a 1 in 80 gradient so care had to be taken when stopping at this station. No 45053, a long-time resident at Inverness and regular Highland line performer, would be no stranger to steep gradients. Recent reports suggest that there is an embryonic preservation site at this station and I wish it every success on the beautiful Galloway coast of southwest Scotland.

Right: Another Derek Cross car, this time the 1961 Sunbeam Alpine which, I think, was his favourite. As a nine year old in the passenger seat I can certainly confirm it went extremely well and chasing steam around Scotland was great fun! The train in the background coming off the Big Water of Fleet Viaduct near Gatehouse of Fleet in the SLS Easter Tour of Scotland on 15 April 1963 is 'Jubilee' No 45588 *Kashmir* on the Dumfries–Stranraer leg. A long-time Blackpool locomotive, *Kashmir* had by 1963 reached Carlisle Kingmoor, its last shed, from which it was withdrawn in 1965. The 'Port Road' was a line rich in substantial structures, with the Big Water of Fleet Viaduct amongst the finest, although at some stage the pillars had had to be rebuilt. Those Galloway hills are wild! Although the railway line has long gone, the viaduct lives on in guide books and is listed as a 'place of interest', that's if you can find it, because again the station at Gatehouse of Fleet was seven miles from the village of the same name.

Left: Photographs of diesels on the Dumfries to Stranraer 'Port Road' are unusual. This is largely because the line closed on 14 June 1965, before steam ended and diesels arrived in southwest Scotland in any numbers. This photograph is of a train many of us did not really want to see, especially Derek, and shows the demolition train returning to Dumfries on the afternoon of 21 May 1968 behind BR/Sulzer diesel No D7620. The line was lifted from Dunragit back towards Maxwellton, which remains as a long industrial siding from Dumfries. The demolition train is pictured on the Stroan Viaduct en route from Creetown to Dumfries.

Below: Running around a brake van by towing it with wire was unusual on British Railways. However, one could argue that because the line was closed it was not a BR line! Pictured at New Galloway on 22 October 1968 is BR/Sulzer Type 2. No D7580, running around the demolition train. The line was closed back in June 1965 and lay disused but intact for three years or more before these somewhat melancholy weekly freights began to run. In the background is the old station where the contractor's 0-4-0 diesel can also be seen. The line was lifted from the Dumfries end and the picture is included as much for its unusual shunting as for a diesel on the 'Port Road' which was very uncommon whilst the line was open.

As if steam in southwest Scotland was not interesting enough in the 1960s, the enlightened Scottish Region Board sanctioned the occasional use of four preserved locomotives. These, all in their pre-Grouping liveries and all beautifully kept at Dawsholm shed (65D) in Glasgow, represented examples from the Great North of Scotland Railway, North British Railway, Caledonian Railway and Highland Railway companies. Here we see the Highland Railway example, Jones Goods 4-6-0 No 103 approaching Hurlford shed (67B) just south of Kilmarnock. Unusually, the Jones Goods is in the company of a normal service locomotive, Caledonian '3F' 0-6-0 of 1899, No 57566 (also now preserved at Aviemore), a local Ayrshire resident. The four preserved engines commonly either worked on their own or with each other but rarely with 'normal' (and dirty) locomotives. In this picture taken in July 1963 the Jones Goods and the Caledonian 0-6-0 had, on account of their maximum five-coach load on the steeply graded Ayrshire/Lanarkshire coalfield branches, been paired together and, mid-tour, are visiting Hurlford for servicing.

This picture was a particular favourite of Derek's and much discussed among his local railway friends. 'Crabs' on passenger turns on Glasgow & South Western lines were not common. Here, however, we see No 42743 (another former Highland lines locomotive, having been based at Perth in the 1950s) heading north away from Mauchline on an empty stock train destined for one of the large coaching stock sidings in Glasgow, which in this case Derek records as Smithy Lye. Empty stock trains on G&SW lines were not common, hence the discussion of why a 'Crab' was unusually heading passenger stock. The lines in the foreground are the link from Mauchline to Ayr via Annbank, used mainly by freight traffic and as a diversionary route if the line to the Ayrshire coast via Kilmarnock was unavailable for any reason. No 42743 had been built in June 1927 and was close to the end of its 35-year life, being withdrawn in December 1962, just six months after the photograph was taken.

Above: Situated 11 miles south of Kilmarnock on the G&SW main line was Brackenhill Junction. This was the junction for the branch to the town of Catrine (population 700) and here we see Ayr-based 'Crab' No 42805 approaching the junction from the Catrine direction in the late afternoon of 12 July 1963. I don't think even the natives of Catrine would mind me describing their town as a very small one. The interesting thing is that it ever had a railway and, perhaps more surprising, that it was still open in 1963, but only just, closing completely on 6 July 1964. The passenger service had ceased as long ago as 3 May 1943. The junction faced north and so once back on the G&SW main line the train would pass through Auchinleck before leaving the G&SW line at Mauchline en route to the large local marshalling yard at Falkland Junction just north of Ayr. Of note in the picture is the magnificent G&SW signal over the second wagon of the train.

Right: Awaiting the 'right away' from the station platform at Catrine, terminus of the short and by then freight-only branch off the G&SW main line at Brackenhill Junction, is the thrice-weekly freight back to Ayr. The passenger service had opened with the line in September 1903 and ceased during the war in 1943. In this view, taken on 26 May 1964, Stanier Class 5 No 45460, very obviously from the front buffer beam an Ayr locomotive (67C), is not going to be taxed at all with eight wagons up to Brackenhill Junction, before going briefly on to the G&SW main line and then on to Ayr, some 17 miles distant. No 45460 was built at Crewe in October 1938 and was a long-time Highland line locomotive based at Perth, before moving to Ayr and eventually being withdrawn just over a year later, on 19 June 1965.

Left: The northern end of the Glasgow & South Western route from Carlisle to Glasgow north of the Cumnocks became an important means of access to the Ayrshire coalfields as well as being a 'main' line. Seen here in the summer of 1962 is 'Crab' No 42916 of Ayr shed approaching Auchinleck from the south with a loaded coal train perhaps from Kirkconnel or Knockshinnoch collieries. The train is destined for Ayr Harbour: after Mauchline, the next station, the train would go down the branch via Annbank to its destination. The home signal the train is restarting from protects the G&SW line from the junction with the branch to Muirkirk (and at that stage Carstairs) which is just out of sight behind the photographer. Also of note, even in 1962, is the somewhat motley rake of coal wagons, including wooden examples evident at the front of the train.

Above: The Caledonian Railway Single No 123 and its two ex-Caledonian coaches on an excursion are pictured near Commondyke in the spring of 1962. No 123 was built by Neilson & Co (works No 3553) in 1886 to its own design to be shown at the Edinburgh International Exhibition. It won the Gold Medal there before passing to the Caledonian Railway. It ran as CR No 123 until 1914 when it was renumbered 1123 in the CR's duplicate list, becoming LMS No 14010 in 1923. When withdrawn in April 1935 it was the last Single in service. On withdrawal it was preserved by the LMS at St Rollox before being restored to main line service by Scottish Region. It took part in the 'Railway Races to the North' in 1888 when it hauled the West Coast services in a competition with the East Coast to be the first to reach the CR signalbox at Kinnaber Junction, and thus be the first to reach Aberdeen. It is now preserved in the Transport Museum at the Kelvin Hall in Glasgow, together with the Great North of Scotland Railway's *Gordon Highlander* and the Highland Railway Jones Goods, all well worth a visit.

Left: Ayrshire had been criss-crossed by a number of essentially freight-only branches for years. Many never saw much traffic or indeed went from anywhere obvious to anywhere obvious! By the early 1960s, during what is now dubbed the Beeching era, time had begun to run out for some of these lines. Pictured on 29 March 1964 on a very picturesque local stone viaduct near Cumnock, on what was locally known as the Cumnock A&C (Ayr and Cronberry) line, is Standard 2-6-0 No 77017 of Hurlford shed in Kilmarnock (67B) on the demolition train. An interesting aspect of the train is the position of the guard, who appears to be riding on the back of the rear wagon. Cumnock at that stage also had a station on the G&SW main line. Today, Cumnock has no station, being one of those closed under Beeching. Other stations on the G&SW however, have reopened, including in the last 10 years nearby New Cumnock, Auchinleck and Sanquhar.

Below: After the through line from Auchinleck Junction to Muirkirk and Carstairs was closed, a stub remained to interchange sidings with the NCB at a small hamlet called Cronberry. Here an NCB branch line took off into the Southern Uplands serving a colliery at Cairnhill. At Cronberry on the morning of 1 December 1971 we see NCB steam locomotive Ayr Area No 1 (Andrew Barclay 0-4-0ST No 2244 of 1947) arriving with loaded wagons for Ayr Harbour, to swap with the empties which have arrived up the BR branch. They have arrived behind English Electric Type 1 (which became Class 20) No D8027 which confirmed the local belief that everything that came to Ayrshire was 'second-hand'! No D8027 was delivered in late 1959 to Hornsey in North London and was withdrawn from Haymarket shed in Edinburgh in 1982. The NCB 'Pug' had already had a longer working life!

Left: The interface between BR and the National Coal Board was an important part of the Ayrshire scene. Day and night there was always activity, always interest and always photographic opportunities. This picture, taken on 1 April 1968 after a spring snow shower, confirms all of this. BR steam had been gone for 18 months but ancient NCB locomotives were soldiering on. Grant Ritchie 0-4-0ST NCB No 23 is taking water in a part of the old BR station at Muirkirk. With BR and NCB wagons both evident, the rear one having left the track, the short train will soon resume its shunting duties at nearby Kames colliery preparing the next loaded coal train for the BR diesel to collect.

Above: Pronunciation of places in Scotland was often not easy but this one, the summit on the G&SW main line between Cumnock and New Cumnock, did take some getting used to. The local pronunciation was 'Porworp'! In the 1960s very early on a summer morning there was a succession of northbound traffic on the G&SW, first freight and parcels, then the two overnight sleeping car expresses from London. (1S24 from St Pancras via Leeds and 1S26 from Euston via Preston), then the 6.10am Annan–Glasgow semi-fast. Pictured on 14 April 1962, an unidentified Stanier Class 5 begins the descent of the grade towards Cumnock, Kilmarnock and eventually Glasgow St Enoch. The fact the locomotive number was not recorded is unusual for Derek, who kept meticulous records on steam locomotives but was less detailed on diesels, often recording them only as 'a diesel' or, if they had turned up instead of an expected steam locomotive, worse — 'a stinker'.

The grade on the southbound line from Mauchline up to Polquap was nine miles at 1 in 150. Pictured very close to the top of the bank and emerging from Blackfaulds Cutting is Glasgow Corkerhill (67A)-allocated Standard Class 5 No 73100. It heads a long southbound mixed freight, the destination being the new marshalling yard at Kingmoor just north of Carlisle. On the left are the once-typical railwaymen's cottage where often permanent way staff lived, more or less on top of the job.

This may go some way towards explaining why, in a number of these pictures taken in the 1960s, the track, ballast, embankments and the fencing all looked in such good condition. There was a real pride in the work undertaken on 'their' own stretch of line then, even though the locomotive does not look to have been near a cleaning cloth for some weeks!

Steam had not been gone a year when this picture was taken at Kirkconnel in September 1967. As was often the case in Ayrshire, the railway station was located very close to the coal mine, this picture being taken from the end of the down platform with the pit behind the locomotives. Earlier in the book I mentioned that many of the diesels that replaced steam were 'second-hand' from English sheds. The

Class 25s depicted here were the exception, as some did come new to Scotland in 1966. We see here No D7599 in the loop on a short southbound Nith Valley freight, whilst sisters Nos D7613 and D7611 wait to shunt the colliery before heading back north to Ayr. Derek was amused that it often took two new and expensive diesels to replace a single 30-year-old 'Crab' that had done the job so well for so long.

Left: The southbound 'Thames-Clyde Express' sets off from its second stop at Kirkconnel on the morning of 12 April 1971. The first stop had been Kilmarnock, followed by Kirkconnel then Dumfries and Carlisle, and so over the Settle & Carlisle to Leeds and ultimately London St Pancras. Even before steam ended in 1966 in southwest Scotland this train had been *the* express over the G&SW line for years and was one of the first to become a regular diesel working. Unusually, the train is headed by an English Electric Type 4, No D241. The more regular motive power for the Thames-Clyde was a 'Peak' class diesel or what became Class 45 or 46.

Below left: Sanquhar, the town with the most exotic name in the Nith Valley, is a place of which photographs are scarce. I would suspect that this is not because the locality of Sanquhar has anything bad about it but because the Drumlanrig Gorge and Carronbridge, with its viaduct, to the south and Kirkconnel to the north afford better photographic opportunities. There are other reasons, however, for selecting this photograph. First, as it was taken on 22 October 1983 it illustrates that the Nith Valley has seen the odd steam train since the official end of steam in Scotland in 1967. Secondly, I suppose any book of the railways of Scotland should have a picture of the country's most famous locomotive, with its relevant name *Flying Scotsman*. (Derek would, I am sure, have preferred a Stanier Pacific as opposed to

the Gresley offering!) 'A3s', however, did operate on the Nith Valley for a brief spell in the early 1960s when their East Coast main line days came to an end; a number were allocated to Leeds Holbeck and worked the Leeds–Glasgow trains. Thirdly and finally, I selected the picture of a northbound SLOA excursion to Ayr for the open day because it was one of the last Derek took, just seven months before he died.

Below: The Kirkcudbright branch was worked mostly by '2Ps' until the advent of more modern tank engines which took over until the branch closed. For many years the 1928-vintage Midland '2P' 4-4-0s had been the mainstay of the local passenger service in and around Dumfries. Dumfries, even in 1961, had local passenger trains to Carlisle, Lockerbie, Glasgow, Stranraer and the Solway coast, specifically to Kirkcudbright. Kirkcudbright was served three times a day on weekdays from Dumfries, the 30-mile journey via Castle Douglas taking 58 minutes. At about this time the '2Ps' gave way to Stanier and Standard tanks, but here we see No 40670 shunting the Kirkcudbright branch train (actually often only one coach) at the north end of Dumfries station. The lines in the background are the G&SW Nith Valley line towards Kilmarnock. No 40670 lasted just a few more months in traffic before being withdrawn in December 1962.

Left: Annan is another location of which there are very few photographs, hence my choice of Class 50 diesels to illustrate this picturesque and typical G&SW station just 8 miles from the English border. On the left passing through the station itself is a diverted Glasgow to Liverpool express (1M27) hauled by an English Electric Class 50 locomotive, No 423, on 23 September 1972 After the demise of steam in 1968 the 'D' prefix that had differentiated diesel from steam was dropped to leave just the locomotive number. Shortly afterwards, a five-digit number became the norm at the request of the computer men from TOPS! — Derek did not approve!

Below: A view of the picturesque viaduct immediately north of the station, where the former G&SW main line crosses the River Annan just before it enters the Solway Firth. During the electrification of the Clyde Valley line over Beattock, the Nith Valley line came into its own as an important diversionary route. Pictured crossing the viaduct on 6 September 1971 is a diverted London to Glasgow express (1S47) hauled by two Class 50 locomotives, Nos 420 and 403.

Left: For the Geordie passengers on their Heads of Ayr to Newcastle (Summer Saturdays only) train their holiday in Scotland has just about 100 yards to go. Pictured is grubby Stanier 'Black 5' No 44955 coming off the G&SW line at Gretna Junction. Within the next 100 yards the G&SW line in quick succession joins the Caledonian main line from Glasgow (via Beattock) and then crosses the River Sark, which marks the border, on a short viaduct and so into England and the crew change at Carlisle Citadel. 1N08 was an interesting working which linked Newcastle and the Northeast with Butlin's holiday camp at Heads of Ayr. Motive power varied enormously, with 'B1s', Class 5s of both LMS and Standard varieties and even the odd early diesel all recorded by Derek during the summer of 1964.

Below left: After two hours and 35 minutes the leisurely journey of a stopping train down the Nith Valley line from Glasgow St Enoch is about to end. Having left Glasgow at 12 noon, the train has stopped nine times and is now on schedule for a 2.44pm arrival at Carlisle Citadel station, a distance of 115 miles having been travelled. Pictured at Gretna Junction where the former Caledonian line over Beattock (in the foreground) joins the G&SW line is Standard Class 5 No 73122.

With no appreciable gradients in the 10 miles between Gretna Junction and Carlisle Citadel, the hard work is done and the crew can take in the views of the Solway Firth as the train enters England, 100 yards ahead. No 73122 had been built at Doncaster in January 1956 and had a working life of just 10 years, all of which was spent in Scotland. It was withdrawn in February 1966.

Below: Virtually all the through trains from the west of Scotland entered England through the border city of Carlisle. In that regard, what went on in Carlisle, particularly in terms of motive power from Carlisle Kingmoor shed (12A), played an important part in the workings of southwest Scotland. Many trains changed engines at Carlisle or attached/detached assisting locomotives. Although not of a Nith Valley train, the picture, taken on 19 August 1967, shows a Dundee–Blackpool train in the platform at Carlisle Citadel station changing engines. The English Electric Type 4 diesel which had brought the train from Dundee has given way to 'Black 5' No 45285, now attached to the train and ready to depart for Blackpool. Both locomotives prove the point by carrying the same reporting number, 1M31 —, one in high tech lit blind form, the other in low-tech chalk!

Index of Locations

Front cover: A pleasant summer's day in June 1964 and Ayr allocated Stanier 'Black 5' No 44977 ambles through typical Ayrshire countryside at Dalrymple Junction.

Back cover: The railway, river Nith and the main road all come together and squeeze through the hills in a formation known locally as Drumlanrig gorge. In the spring of 1970 Brush Type 4 No D1991 heads a block train for ICI from Ardeer, in Ayrshire to Haverton Hill on Teesside.